eye

In her 1983 volume of poetry, *Laser Treatment*, Elizabeth Goldring creates vivid word images. In her 2002 volume, *Eye*, the images become a part of the words themselves. The English word *poet* derives from the Greek word ποειν, meaning "to create," and this latest work reveals Elizabeth Goldring at her creative best.

Ms. Goldring's poetry and artistic expressions are deeply personal, but she reveals and expresses universal human emotions in her creations. Descriptions such as "lobsters" floating in her view and laser treatments being nailed "one nail at a time" define powerful images in her early work, as Ms. Goldring was actively suffering from ongoing visual changes from her diabetes. In this new work, vision again is the overriding theme. This new work, however, finds Ms. Goldring adjusted to her loss of vision and actually using her low vision as an artistic tool for herself and for us. In these latest creations, as the images become words themselves, this volume treats us to vivid word images as well as innovative image words.

In *Eye* Ms. Goldring has met her visual challenge and fashioned an artistic and intellectual conquest.

—Jerry Cavallerano, OD, PhD, &
Lloyd M. Aiello, MD
Beetham Eye Institute, Joslin Diabetes Center,
Harvard University

e y e

poems
&
retina prints

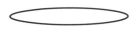

Elizabeth Goldring

BkMk Press
University of Missouri - Kansas City

BkMk Press
University of Missouri - Kansas City
5101 Rockhill Road
Kansas City, MO 64110
(816) 235-2558 (voice)
(816) 235-2611 (fax)
bkmk@umkc.edu
http://www.umkc.edu/bkmk

MAC
MISSOURI ARTS COUNCIL

Financial assistance for this project has been provided by the
Missouri Arts Council, a state agency.
Thanks to MIT Museum & Center for Advanced Visual Studies
Cover Design: Ananda Leininger
Cover Illustration: *Face of the Dragonfly*, 2001, 16 1/2 x 30 in.
Book Design: Susan L. Schurman
Managing Editor: Ben Furnish
Thanks also to Michael Nelson, Gloria Vando, Jeri Keimig, Jessica
Hylan, Dika Eckersley, Sherry Cromwell-Lacy & Beryl Rosenthal
Author Photo: Otto Piene
Printing: Josten's, Topeka, Kansas

Library of Congress Cataloging-in-Publication Data

Goldring, Elizabeth
   Eye : poems, retina prints / ElizabethGoldrin
      p. cm.
    ISBN 1-886157-37-5 (Paperback)
   1. People with visual disabilities--Poetry. 2. Vision--Poetry.
   I. Title.
    PS3557.03846 E94 2002
    811'.54--dc21

                        2002007316

CONTENTS

EROS AMBULANCE

PORTRAITS AND DIALOGUES

RETINA PRINTS

蜻蛉の顔は大かた眼玉かな

知足

The face of the dragon-fly
Is practically nothing
But eyes.

–Chisoku

For my parents,
my daughter, Jessica,
and my husband, Otto

ACKNOWLEDGMENTS

Prairie Schooner: "Prairie Schooner Portfolio" for including 10 Retina Prints and "Rosemary," "Harry," "Driving Down to Nice," "Swansong," "Wildflowers," "Hugs and Kisses," Lavender," and "Neo-Wilhelmians."

Ananda Leininger, MIT '04, for her important contribution to cover design and the Retina Prints.

MIT Museum, particularly Beryl Rosenthal and Don Stidson, and MIT Council for the Arts for making an exhibition of Retina Prints and poems possible to coincide with the publication of *Eye* .

UROP (Undergraduate Research Opportunities Program) at MIT for providing ongoing support to the Visual Language for the Blind Project.

Syllabus, which published a set of Retina Prints in Goldring's article "Seeing for People who are Blind or Visually Challenged".

Rob Webb, Senior Scientist, Schepens Eye Institute, Harvard Unversity, inventor of the scanning laser opthalmoscope and collaborator on the Visual Language Project.

Dr. Lloyd Aiello, Chief, and Dr. Jerry Cavallerano, Beetham Eye Institute, Joslin Diabetes Center, Harvard University.

Stephen A. Benton, Allen Professor and Director, and Otto Piene, Director Emeritus, Center for Advanced Visual Studies, MIT.

Cannon USA for the loan of the SLO used in production of the Retina Prints.

THE RETINA PRINTS
An Explanatory Note

The Retina Prints are based on analog video captures of the retina (the back of the eye) looking at or absorbing visual information—faces, words, landscapes, etc. The Scanning Laser Ophthalmoscope (SLO) is the diagnostic medical instrument that scans visual information onto the retina. It also records the retina looking. Images of the "looking retina" are then digitized, "painted" (in Photoshop) and eventually printed on a large format plotter-printer.

My impulse to make Retina Prints and to use the SLO as a "seeing machine" was precipitated by a remarkable experience. Several months after I became blind, with only light and shadow perception in both eyes, I was given a test to determine the degree of remaining retina function in each eye. The diagnostic tool used was the SLO which projected "stick figure" images onto selected areas of my retinas. When I discovered that I could actually *see* some of the test pictures I asked if I could try a word—the word *sun*. I could see it, too. It was the first word I had been able to read for a long time. For me, a writer who was beginning to forget the shape of words, this was truly a significant moment.

Almost since that day I have been experimenting with the SLO. I use it as a "seeing machine" for my right eye which still has residual retina function but no useful vision. In collaboration with the SLO inventor and physicians, scientists, engineers, artists and students at MIT and Harvard, I am attempting to create visual experiences and poetry for people who have low vision or no sight at all. To avoid visual confusion and frustrating " white noise," I believe that visual communication for people with impaired sight should rely on the same principles of economy and intensity that guide my poems—saying a lot with as few strokes as possible. I select imagery that I find evocative and provocative.

My fascination with the technology lies in being able to transport my art and poetry to places where it might otherwise not be seen or received. My dream is that one day people who are blind will be able to enjoy internet access to public buildings, distant landscapes, faces of loved ones as well as the words and glyphs of poetry. In 1996, at MIT we hooked up an SLO to the internet and the world of virtual reality. I am optimistic that adapting virtual environments to low vision needs will become an important use of virtual reality

For me the Retina Prints are visual poems. They are also a by-product of my experiments with the SLO. Each retina "animated" by the octopus-like tendrils of the optic nerve is as individual as a thumb print. The words and images projected onto my damaged retinas with the SLO, retain an indelible "after-image" quality that I celebrate with the Prints. (The SLO is a black and white /gray-scale system, so the color is assigned.)

Perhaps, because I am visually challenged, what I see spirits my writing more than ever. For me The Retina Prints are traces of a laborious experience of seeing–memories of woven images and words "sitting on my retina"–sometimes only palpable through the SLO. Once seen and captured they are indelible –Retina Prints.

GOING AWAY

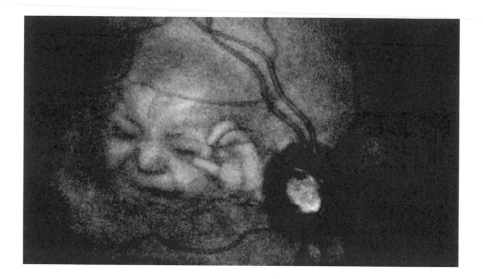

Womb (Serafina at 3 Weeks on her Father's Retina),
2001, 15 x 26 1/4 in.

SITTING FOR A PORTRAIT
At La Gavina in S'Agaro, Spain

The sun falls directly on me.
 Shadows fall on me directly, too

I am composed of pure sun
and wrought iron,
graffiti
stamped on my ruined retina.

At owl's light I'm colors of clay.

UNOBTRUSIVE EROTIC ARCHITECTURE

To see or not,
the clay onion
pushing up through grasses,
flaunting itself gently against sky.
It falls back
lowered into hairy shadows,
nests of leaves and
waving palm fronds.

Over there
another onion rises
full,
white.

DISCOVERING MOGADOR
where,
in the 16th century,
there was a factory
for manufacturing royal purple
from spiny murex shells.

Black is to white
as dark is to light
and night
to sun
no solids.

My mirages are flat.

This light
builds a town
paints angles
rounds a blue corner.

Islands puncture distance
bright with forts.

As we drive to Agadir
The snow-capped Atlas
clouds on ocean,
lines of breakers
glass   green.

DRIVING THE MOROCCAN COAST IN EARLY SPRING

A torrent of white light
long as the coves and breakers
tears loose from pine and
tarragon-tufted hills.

On the off side:
the architecture of towns
(topless shoeboxes)
and clay,
red
with agriculture.

ON RETURNING TO TAROUDANT

Everything's still sugared,
tea
orange juice
yogurt.
Our taxi driver speeds off
without giving us a receipt
because he can't write.
At the hotel
people lie around the pool
striking national poses.
The cat's back
clatter of plates
cooing doves
the way light meanders
through openings and shadows.

Le traité de soir,
black sky pinned with stars.

Four am duets of morning cocks
and muezzin.

LAVENDER

Did Hegel say
r e d
is absolute?
No,
it's *lavande*
in Senanque
where the auras of all color
vibrate
deep as the throat of a mocking bird.

And oils
spill hot shine,
flow
purple.

A nun crosses the field,
her fluttering habit
a lunar bird.

Snow, 1996-2002, 25 3/4 x 35 in.

DRIVING DOWN TO NICE

I remember
the four a.m. flowers
the fresh scents
the closed air of the car,
how red sun
filled the blue morning
as we drove down to Nice,
and how s h e came up
over the knobbed hairy tit mountain
(the citron sorbet in Cassis
with lemon rind pressed in it)
the sun
burned black at the center,
orange
opening into yellow
(the taste of lemon rind).

As we drove into Nice
I felt the earth shake
and the bitter aftershocks
as shadows of the black sun
crossed your eyes
clouding the lavender fields
back at Senanque,
stifling songs of *missa solemnis*
still hot in my gut.

HERBS TANGLED WITH AUTUMN
A Provence Diary

One.
You cut your toenails for three days

We say nothing,
thoughts jumping between us.

(It's quiet without sunflowers and lavender.)

Dry air passes through mist and fog.
Fires smoke like geysers at the horizon.

A new highway has swallowed Beaumettes,
gas station and all.

You were bothered by a little paper
caught in your new socks,
didn't know what it was.

Two.

We swam for nearly an hour.
You did 15 rounds.

At times your breaths come heavy,
at times you seem fit without trying.

We smell mint-after-rain
by St.Véran
where cicadas are still chanting.

Our vitamins are running low.

BEIJING

Down a wide street
metal blur assails me,
sun
glinting white
on spokes,
white shirts.

Food smells
simmer in vats of peanut oil,
gold and red
of pineapple and watermelon.

Styrofoam trash
floats on heads of a billion green flies.

At the temple of the sun
perfect clouds
sit in the biggest sky ever.
On the sidelines
cypress
twist to shape words,
whispered calligraphy.

Ancient as gold and lotus
cypress cajole from the sidelines
like old men playing cards.

At the university
Art, Beauty, Truth,
a lecture
yelled from oversized pages

simultaneous translations,
no questions.

THE UGLY FISH

> *mer*
> clear   blue
>   light
> chlorophyl of pine

Off shore
a man had a heart attack
while fishing,
just made it back.

They used our friend's mobile phone
to call the hospital in Split,
drove him
through the mile long, one -way tunnel
to Jelsa,
helicoptered him from there.

That night
in Ivan Dolac,
we ate ugly fish
—rascasse—
bane of divers.
Backed into caves
underwater
they beat their fins
like wings.

This morning the father
of the man who died
last night
takes this boat out
as usual.

The funeral procession:

men in white shirts
narrow black ties,
the purple-frocked priest
swinging incense,
wreaths of flowers
bright with sunlight
bearing the fisherman's casket
uphill.

DALMATIAN BEACH, 1996

Charred
shoals,

black as shining sun
on deep water,

black as sun
shining
on rape
murder
bitter grief,

white ships
and Adriatic
blue.

DUBROVNIK, 1996

From the ramparts:
fresh blood of new roofs

centuries of torment
locked in stone.

> In Nebraska
> voices carried by clouds
> evaporated with clouds.
> Wheat held cries of strangulation
> only a moment
> before they turned to wind.

On the prairie
pain was not immortal.

GOING HOME

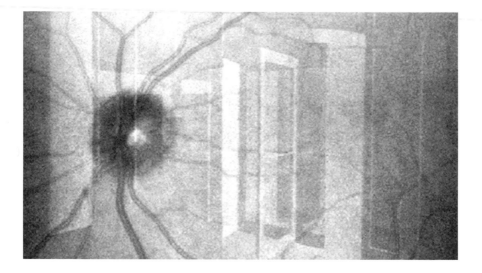

Revolving Door on Rodin's Retina, 2000, 15 x 26 1/4 in.

CIGAR TREE
(Things aren't what they seem.)

A leaf surfaces in the pool
swimming like a frog.
The ochre stones of the mending wall
look like our old dog
hunkering down.
One cloud eats another.

Poppies
red in eyes
still drowsy with today's early light.

BITTERSWEET

From the top of the hill
muted colors this year,
even the maple reds.
Up close
their veins throb
ox-blood.

Bittersweet
threatens our silos.

Aging purples of raspberry,
cut branches
ready to burn.

My eyes waver
as veils of my winter
curtain this view.

Against my panes
first cicles form
lengthening daggers.

Descent, 2001, 19 1/4 x 30 in.

INDIAN SUMMER

I was sitting on our bed
between the golden rainbows
when he told me.
Now they were certain.
Every bone,
every piece of cartilage
came loose.
My body,
a bird
struggling to keep in air.

I don't even know
precisely
where the prostate is.

WILD FLOWERS

Daisies, dianthus
and phlox
outdo the planted perennials.
Stars
unframed in the wheatfields
wild,
unpainted.
Here and there a wizened carcass,
or a snake
looking like a stick in the grass.
I want to pick these fields for you,
bring them into the barn
where you are painting
blue women.

Blue Light, 2001, 32 x 53 1/8 in.

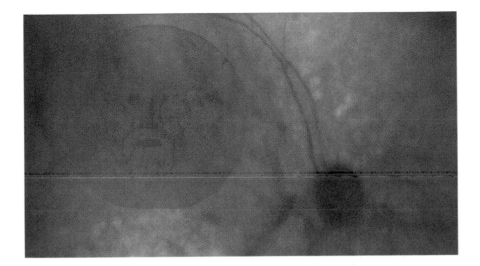

Bocca dela Verita´ on Goldring's Retina,
2001, 22 3/8 x 40 in.

SEACHANGE

Leaves whirled through the air
like flocks of lost birds.
We already watched TV at 11 am
waiting for noon and the Beef and Ale
Bloody Marys
Cape Codders
our usual winter fare of double dogs.
In the storm's aftermath
scattered songs.
A few words
clinging to trees
labor to fly.

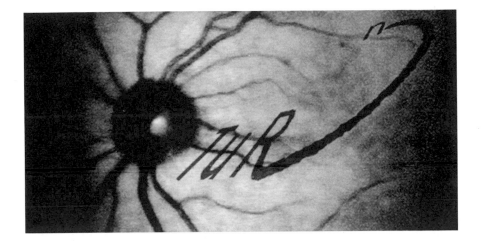

Turn *on Retina*, 2001, 16 1/4 x 32 in.

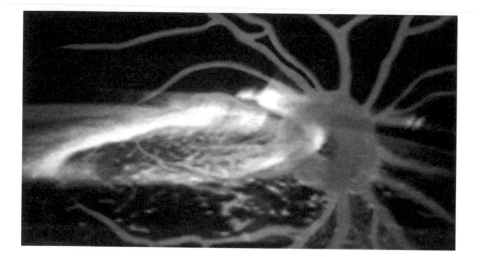

Aurora from Inner Space, 2001, 15 1/4 x 28 in.

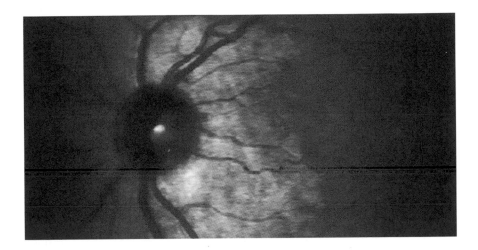

Glowing Retina, 2001,20 5/8 x 40 in.

GOING HOME

I wonder if it's all still there:

pale lights of fireflies caught in jars

Dutch elm disease and the ringing of trees
up and down Rathbone Road

tornadoes and twisters
that took the roofs off houses
at the edge of town

headlights drowning in streets
flooded by Antelope Creek
just a block from our meat locker
and the house with Jesus Saves
painted all over the outside walls.

A high wire cage
fenced deer
and remaining bison
so we could feed them bread.

We passed the fall-out shelter
every day at noon
on our way to Van Dorn Drugs
and the in-ground trampoline.

After several of us got hurt
it was removed as a hazard
like they took away the x-ray machine downtown
where we could watch the bones of our toes
turn green inside new shoes.

At Miller and Paine's foundation shop
I got measured for my first brassiere
the summer
the asphalt sank
beneath my new spiked heels
(3 1/2 inch red pattens)
and we all saw
Pillow Talk and *Gidget Goes Hawaiian.*

During the polio epidemic
we stayed away from circuses, gutters,
county fairs and public swimming pools.
When Nancy came down with it
we tried to get her to walk again.
She was the bravest girl I knew.

We pretended her wheelchair was our getaway car.

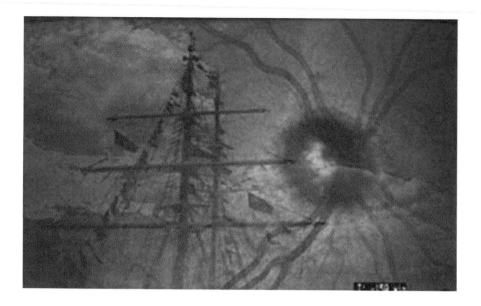

Tall Ships on Naveem's Retina, 2000, 18 1/4 x 30 in.

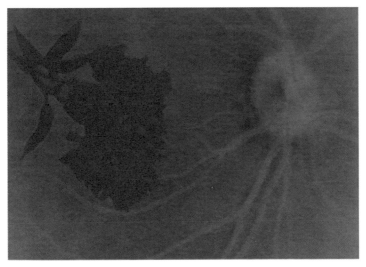

Peony Afterglow, 1999, 22 x 14 1/4 in.

MULTICULTURAL
Düsseldorf

The fast food chef
feeds his shrine.
"Must drink tea, each day,"
he says.

"Won-ton soup?"
I nod.
In German I ask him how he is.
"No good,"
he replies in English.
"I must sleep alone."

I don't tell him
how sad it makes me too,
in case
It's a proposition.

THE CASKET SHOP*

The casket shop on Hüttenstrasse
once sold cheap flowers,
before that, maternity clothes.
It caters to a local clientele,
German, Greek and Portuguese.

Grain and carved wood coffins
laid out spaciously
suggest elbow room in the "upper room".
Store fluorescence shines so even
there's never an electric glitch,
no shadows.

A young couple
arms linked
walk between the boxes
as if they are cars.

A middle-aged man, hands clasped,
bows his head.
A pencil-nose woman with a Sistine smile,
perhaps she pictures her husband of 50 years
couched not in front of TV,
but in one of the beds
she would provide.

Lights up and down the street go off.
Lingering spots illuminate the cost.
You can get a basic box for just 200 DMark
or you can customize your casket
with photographs, poems, trinkets of life

*(a practice almost Egyptian).

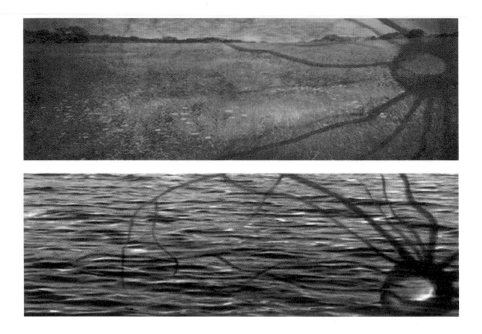

Fields, 2001, 20 5/8 x 30 in.

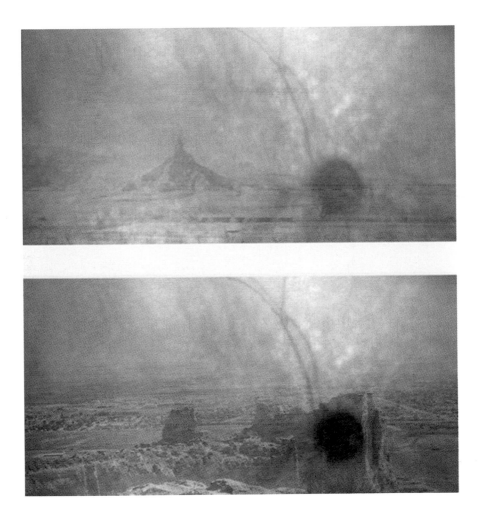

Nebraska on Goldring's Retina, 2001, 27 x 25 in.

FLEAS

My eyes reveal
faint scraps of lace and
dusty baubles.

Who wore them
passed them on to daughters
hid them from a greedy aunt?

Brooches
clipped to hearts
clasped in hands
reflecting colors of eyes,
the shape of a tear.

Among bric-a-brac and
foam rubber stomachs
a mother's postcards from her son,

once scrutinized by Hitler's men,
standard words
saying nothing that could not be said

read
again and again.

Ingie hopes I won't bargain for a fertility mask
riddled with maggots.
She's collecting lace and
white soup tureens.

MASS PIKE WEST

A shaft of light
descends from a cloud
at sunset.

I bump along
heading West
expecting emotion
to pop in my head.

Six hours
plus three hours
equals nine hours
to Cairo.

Here,
it's leap year.

Eye, 1998, 20 5/8 x 30 in.

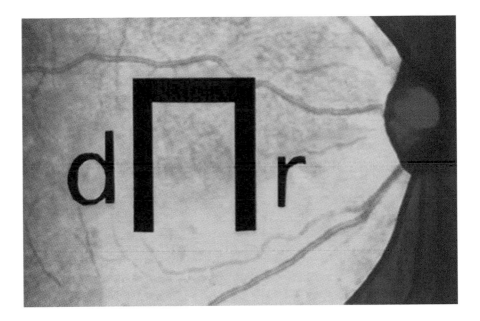

Door *on Sabrina's Retina*, 1998, 22 x 33 1/8 in.

STATE CAPITOL
BOSTON, MA
Climbing Beacon Hill from Park Street Station

Today,
Bulfinch's old girl
freezes the sky
like a martini
ice cube.

SARDINES

In a fish tank
on the fast train to Pasadena
all sardines swim in the same direction.
When one turns
all follow.

One said we'd live to be 100
and should prepare.
Another said at the rate we're destroying the environ-
ment
 it will be our last decade on earth.
A third said in 50 years there'll be no such thing as
Groton
or a farm in Groton.
We'll all be living in space.

Due to an accumulation of snow
the Institute closed at 2 p.m.
All non-essential personnel were asked to leave.
When the meeting broke up
roads out of town were nearly impassable.

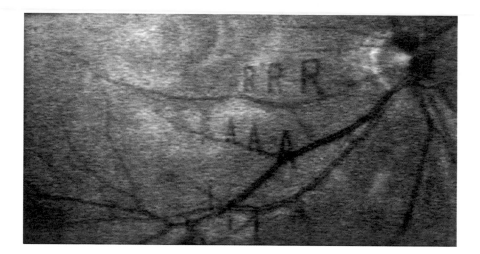

Rain *on Min-Hank's Retina*, 1998, 16 x 30 in.

Eye to Eye (Elizabeth Goldring on Otto Peine's Retina),
1999, 22 x 27 1/2 in.

AT THE UNIVERSITY
There are two pools,
one for the fast lane, cutaway jerks,
the other for the laidback swimmer.

I'm floating.
A hard dive slaps the shallow water.
I turn.
One of them has thrust himself into my pool.
He flashes,
jumps out
smiling.

Real swimmers piss in shallow water,
relief from combat lapping in the other pool.
(It's chemically treated , of course.)

Goggles taut,
muscles flexed,
another swimmer strikes.
He too
comes up smiling.

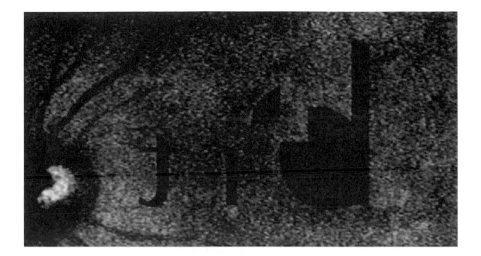

Bit, 1997-2001, 18 x 33 1/4, 33 x 61

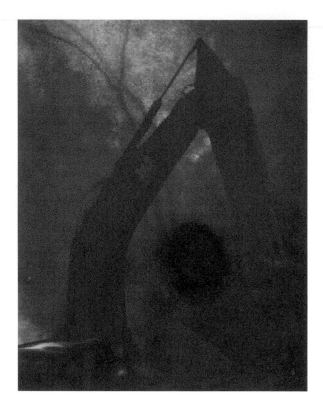

Shovel, 2000, 15 1/2 x 12 in.

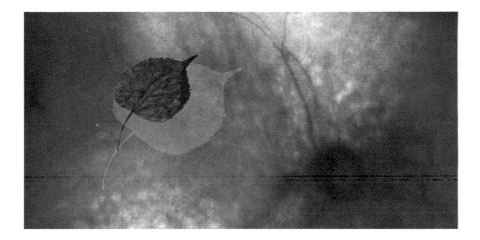

September Eleven, 2001, 20 x 40 in.

NEO-WILHELMIANS

the ones who
drop their briefcases
on your foot
with a crisp smack
slam the bins shut
in unison
with a loud clap.
They are nasty and mean
short-haired and clean
these neo-wilhelmian
not so gentle men
asserting themselves in business
bang bidi bang
bidi bang bang bang.
They eat sweets though
and their time is now.

CAGED
Waiting for a bus at the Cambridge Common

Everything looks steady
and fine
along the lines of picket fences.

A stream of AAAAAAAA

Schools belch
jumbling crosswalks.

Good eye
reconstructs
blue and stammering
white.

A giant bellows
wheezes

mmmmmmmmmmmmmm

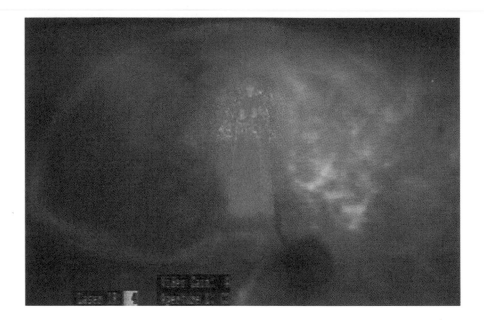

Murano Virgin on Goldring's Retina, 2002, 21 1/4 x 32 in.

EROS
AMBULANCE

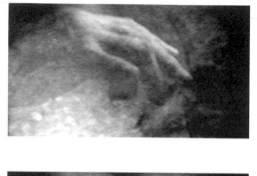

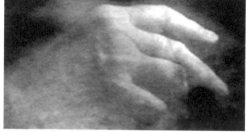

Hand Eye Coordinates, 1999, 7 1/2 x 6 in.

EROS AMBULANCE SERVICE

Role call
to all
crazy, sick,
dying.

Skidding through October fires
Eros burns rubber.
He chases naked light
onto naked windows

catches
women
in
free
fall.

Wrists white
fingers
reaching
Oh,
how we
bleed.

DIAMOND-STUDDED FEET

A piece of glass lodges in my foot
　　or is it a diamond?

The masseuse didn't see it
although she does my feet.
My husband didn't see it.

My foot isn't c　u　t
or　b　l　o　o　d　y.
A　　d　i　a　m　o　n　d
sits there like a pretty object.

The doctor removes it
presents it to me
like a ringbearer.
It slips off his tray
gets　l　o　s　t.

Diamond　　p　i　t
(sitting pretty, like an object).

Mud stuck to wedding vows
dries　　　glowing.

SWANSONG

Migrations flock
intensify
April's coronations
Blue swans rising,
their breasts pressed together
like thumbs
praying.

Swanclouds
converge
l i f t
evaporate
leaving windswept legs in sand.

Swans ascend,
our hands
their traces.

MEDITATIONS

Your words,
worn shoes.
I stumble over them at night.
By day,
open sky
green earth,
the great Buddha bullfrog.

HARRY

Old man
white thistle
sagging jowls
plays the Jacaranda
where he used to play
mainstage
trombone.

It's his birthday.

I say I can't see to dance.
He looks at me
like he won't believe.
Dancing me
Into the waves

He said   g   o   o   d,
slid his trombone.

Til 3 am
we danced.
Time to time
he   b l e w   o u t.

Next day
he sent me fifty roses
curled
with yellow
edges.

A POET'S BATH

Water
Filling a sarcophagus
bathes
the poet.
Languishing
she idles,
purrs.
Eyes glaze.
Leopard lips bloom,
a sneer.
She scissors sentences apart,
trims vowels to rodent cries.
Her poems,
lost rosettas
naked swimmers
soap giraffes
without necks.

TRAINSPOTTING

Waiting's the essence of all feeling.

 A train ride may be thirty-five minutes long
but anticipation can precede it by days.

It's still early.
I'm already at the station.

I wonder if she'll appear as she said in her phone call,
minutes after I expected the ring.

In last night's dream she failed to show up.
 Trains horn the distance

 As I wait, in full view of platform and street
  a man swings in on crutches
  I finger a wad of chewing gum under the bench

Maybe she'll come by car.

A DIALOGUE

Nurse:
"Your wife looks tired."

"Yes,
she's sick and tired,
nervous
too."

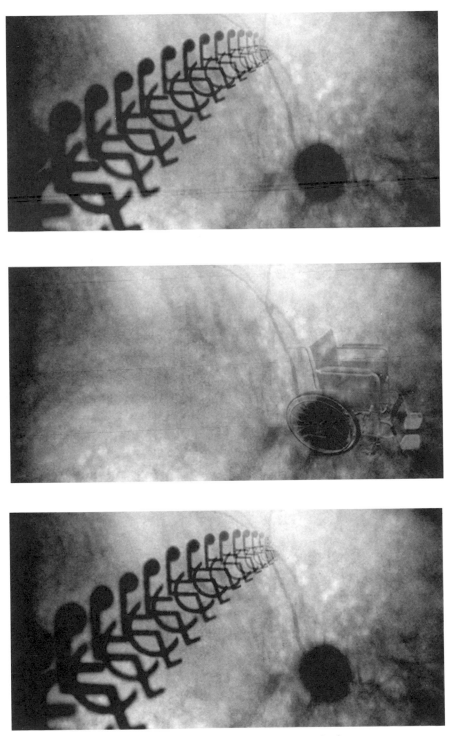

Logos (3), 2001, 18 x 36; 24 x 55 3/4 in.

REACTION

I drank cranberry juice
still sweated
drank coke, you came in.
I told you I needed sugar.
You poured me bright colored candies from a jar
unwrapped kisses
from your secret stash.
I can't get rid of the taste of lilac
wish it was ice cream.

ROSEMARY

The pot of
dead rosemary is heavy.
Its dry twigs
smell sweeter than ashes
as I carry the urn
outside.

CLOCKWORK

Dying's like clockwork.
We think it'll be different,
we'll beat the odds
but there are other factors
not in our favor.

Your spirit's wound tight.
Your clockface,
a snow ball
coming.

PORTRAITS
AND
DIALOGUES

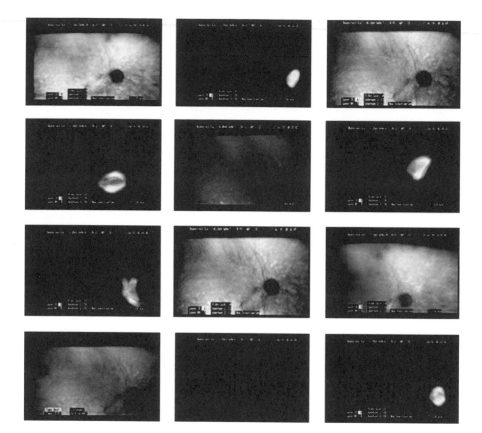

Poets' Eyes (Constance Merritt and Elizabeth Goldring),
2002, 29 3/4 x 32 in.

FOR CAMILLE

It always rains at the Musée Rodin in Paris.

GARDEN STATE

It's 8:30 a.m.
at a service plaza
off the Jersey Turnpike.
A waitress calls across the restaurant:

"You cain't set down there,
s 'already been purified,
disinfected fer dinner."

"You cain't pump yer own gas neether
not in the state of New Joisey
you cain't,"
the filling station attendant informs us.

"A couple of months back
someone tried it
right here. "

"Got hisself arrested,
he did.
Even his lawyer couldn't get him off.

On our way out
we pass puffing Elizabeth,
last whiff of the "Garden State."

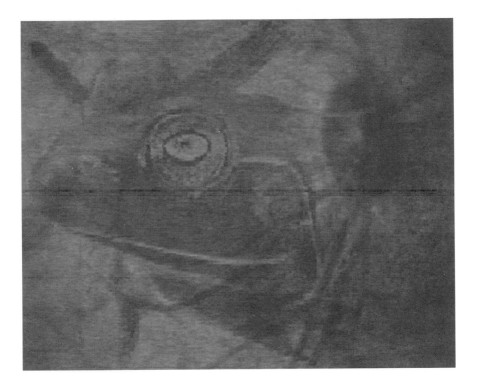

Frogpond, 1999, 22 x 27 1/4; 33 x 60 in.

(*for Dan Jaffe*)
He's
RECONSTRUCTING DAN
he said.

I always saw him
whole.
Wide hat
pushed back,
he's off to Florida
for good.
Eyes squinting
downturned at the corners,
casting about for
a new tune,
a fresh soul,
the next poem.

NO SMOKING PLEASE
(*for Daddy's 80th Birthday*)

Where are your pipes?
chewed black
cherry bowls,
puffed clouds of smoke,
logo for your TV show
on the West.

You packed them away
so carefully
in that shoebox tied with string,
said you'd get them out again
once you retired.

Reason glowed in your hands.

You admonished me
for stripping birch bark off a tree.
Before it was politically correct.
you showed us the shame of Pine Ridge.

While you beheld Vesuvius
 and Popocatepetl close up,
Chinese poppies, too,
I took off for Paris
fuming Gauloises.

So far
 no smoldering tobacco
escapes beneath your study door.
But you have yet to retire
your final work
still   in   draft.

        read at The Four Seasons Restaurant, New York City,
        January 23, 1997

ROOT CANAL

Black and blue chairs
bruise white space.
Philodendron
grope the corners.

Clients
leaf through magazines.
On the wall
Albers' squared tooth.

These guys are ART collectors.

My name
(misread…)

The lozenge recliner
masked hobbits
Interior gardens
(endodontists
in golf carts
chipping.)

My roots marshall themselves like mangroves.
"You have a small mouth,"
he says.
Two clicks,
novacaine's in.

After an hour's perfidy
he informs me
he's found only two roots.
There are three.
I must return next week.

(Aborigines
spit out rotten teeth,
decorate their mouths
with shells.)

DYNAMIC SPLINT

My arm careened like a drunk
flinging itself in all directions.
The nurse caught it,
handed it back to me.

The anesthesiologist told me
She used to live in New Mexico
(fires out there
started at Bandelier
hands burning
reaching out of flames).
From the other side of the sheet
the surgeon said he 'd send the diseased cells
to Canada
for analysis.

My splint is blue and white
rigged with wheels and rubber bands.

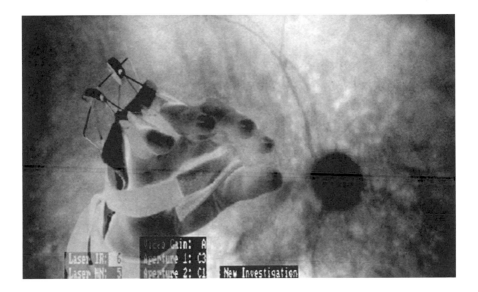

Goldring's Dynamic Splint on her Retina, 2000,
9 x 14 3/4 in.

GLORIA
(for Gloria Vando)

She didn't mind
my new year's greeting
(the poem about a coffin shop)
though many of her friends are dying
(it's the season).
She didn't mind.
Already
she'd gotten pictures of tires,
skinned rabbits
(it's the season).

She says
the trouble with her doctor is
he doesn't have a sense of humor.

TIP AND ZIB TRIPS
for Tippy (Phillip) Dow

I was seven when you were ten.
You were my friend then:

We wrote letters in invisible ink
grew Chinese flowers in the sink
made necklaces from fireflies
invented perfect lies.

On the Dow's front porch
we played Simon Lagree.
The old elm
was our home free.

We sent away for pamphlets and maps
scavenged Mission Orange bottle caps.
Our turtles got lost in the house.
Their names were Flower
and Fledermaus.

You gashed my finger by mistake,
chased me with leeches
around Leech Lake.

                ❖   ❖   ❖   ❖   ❖

You died while I was in Leipzig,
the week they razed the Wall.

We started a travel agency
Back in Lincoln, Nebraska
(when I was seven
and you were ten.)

I've beamed you
—via interplanetary rover—
the latest revisions of the map
of Berlin.

Here's to small dreams,
my friend!

Full*on Goldring's Retina*, 1997-2001, 20 x 20 in.

HUGS and KISSES

I hug the sour-face
middle-age lady
her dyed yellow hair
pinned up in rollers.
I beg her to tell me
what she remembers
of love.
The joy,
the ache of it,
the longing
when it was raw
as the new skins of my lacerated hand.

BAER

Night settles.
We start out
guided by our shoes,
missing our dog.

Tin rain
falls from trees in the forest.
Ice pelts our necks.

(melting onslaught
trinkets of siege
nights of hoary tin men
looking for dogs
more firing
too late for music)

If this had been summer rain
night would not have touched ground
and Baer
deaf to Gabriel's trumpets
would live.

(tin bones
raining from trees in the forest
rifle antics of hunters)

We never saw
his flimsy rag of a body
bouncing in the back of the pick-up
over these icy roads.

STRANGERS

He plays the piano
loud
relentless
She doesn't like the shawl
He plays all arpeggios
staccato
Chords get lost

She leaves it in her closet
doesn't send it back
A sip of wine
blue glass
He says he never plays "Strangers in the Night"
He always plays "Strangers"
The shawl is green

her eyes
strangers
Every night
I hear that tune
Green's the color of your eyes too
when you're gleaming mad

Now she's married.

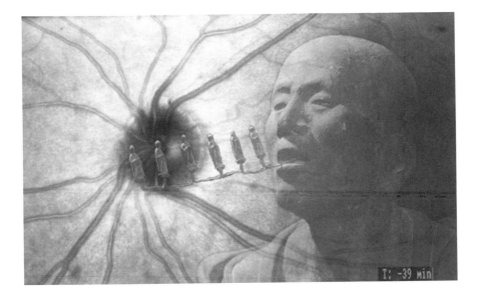

Wandering Monk, Kyoto, on Ananda's Retina, 2002,
16 7/8 x 30 in.

ALLEGRO
A Mother's Lullaby

When she was a baby
her ears stuck out.
When she laughed
we all laughed too.
Matted black curls pasted to that perfect head
born cesarean, five weeks ahead of time,
Oh, how she screamed.
Now she's up there onstage
beyond the orchestra.
I hear her voice
(her first scream).
Among shadows onstage
a group of maidens.
I know it's she.

Out of these old joints
and off key spirit
this body angel sings.

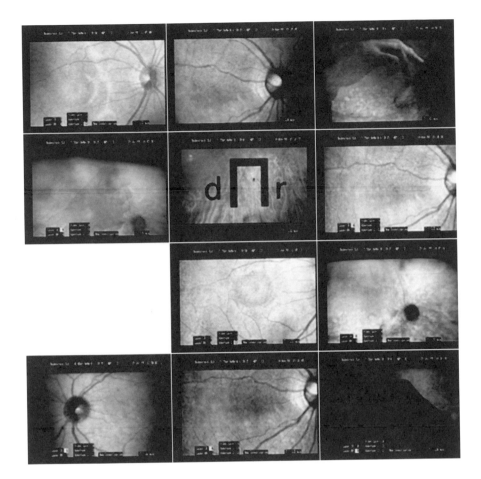

Visual Language, 2000, 33 7/8 × 33 3/4 in.

UND WÜNCHEN EINEN GUTEN FLUG
(Kommoedchen, Düsseldorf)

c a b a r e t
m a r c h e s !
I understand the words,
sometimes:
fresh clipped drums
rat a tat tat
rat a tat tat
coughed
against the smokey
c a b a r e t
my daugheter sings.
she puffs but doesn't
breathe in,
tilts her head
and laughs.

She's my daughter
not his
but she's learned his songs
the way
I never could.

Additional Prints in MIT Exhibition

Eye Dance, 1999-2002, 21 x 37 in.
Eye, 1996-2002, 21 1/2 x 40 in.
Face, 1996-2002, 20 3/4 x 38 in.
Eye to Eye (Otto Piene on Elizabeth Goldring's Retina),
1999, 21 x 28 in.

Elizabeth Goldring's books include *Laser Treatment* (Blue Giant Press) and *Without Warning* (Helicon Nine Editions & BkMk Press). She has co-authored *Centerbeam* with Otto Piene (MIT Press) as well as *The Sky Art Conference* (MIT Press). *Prairie Schooner* published a group of her poems and Retina Prints in 2001. In her current research, she seeks a means to visualize vision loss and to create visual language and a poetry of visual experiences for people like herself whose sight is limited.

Goldring's videotapes include "The Inner Eye From the Inside Out" with Vin Grabill, "A Visual Language for the Blind" with Rob Webb, and "Eye Dance" with Seth Riskin.

She has presented her poetry, multimedia environments and installations at venues in Europe and North America. With Otto Piene, she co-directs the International Sky Art Conference, an ongoing series of conferences and events directed toward humanist and aesthetic explorations of sky and space.

Goldring is the Charlotte Moorman Senior Fellow at MIT's Center for Advanced Visual Studies, where she has also served as acting co-director and exhibits and projects director as well as lecturer in architecture.

Her poems, photographs and writings have appeared in such publications as *Asylum, Spud Songs, Parnas, Leonardo, New England Journal of Optometry,* and *Syllabus. ABC Evening News* with Peter Jennings, the BBC, and *New Letters on the Air* with Angela Elam are some of the media venues where she has been interviewed about her work.

Goldring graduated cum laude from Smith College and received an M.Ed. from Harvard University. She lives with her husband, Otto Piene, in Groton, Massachusetts, and Düsseldorf, Germany.